ESTJ: Understanding &
Relating with the Guardian
MBTI Personality Types Series

By: Clayton Geoffreys

Table of Contents

Foreword

Have you ever been curious about why you behave certain ways? Well I know I have always pondered this question. When I first learned about psychology in high school, I immediately was hooked. Learning about the inner workings of the human mind fascinated me. Human beings are some of the most impressive species to ever walk on this earth. Over the years, one thing I've learned from my life experiences is that having a high degree of self-awareness is critical to get to where you want to go in life and to achieve what you want to accomplish. A person who is not self-aware is a person who lives life blindly, accepting what some label as fate. I began intensely studying psychology to better understand myself, and through my journey, I discovered the Myers Brigg Type Indicator (MBTI), a popular personality test that distinguishes between sixteen types of individuals. I hope to cover some of the most prevalent personality types of the MBTI test and share my findings with you through a series of books. Rather than just reading this for the sake of reading it though, I want you to reflect on the information that will be shared with you. Hopefully from reading *ESTJ: Understanding & Relating with the Guardian*, I can pass along some of the abundance of information I have learned about ESTJs in general, how they view the world, as well as their greatest strengths and weaknesses. Thank you for purchasing my book. Hope you enjoy and if you do, please do not forget to leave a review! Also, check out my website at claytongeoffreys.com to join my exclusive list where I let you know about my latest books. To thank you for your purchase, you can go to my site to download a free copy of *33 Life Lessons: Success Principles, Career Advice & Habits of Successful People.* In the book, you'll learn from some of the greatest thought leaders of different industries on what it takes to become successful and how to live a great life.

Cheers,

Clayton Geoffreys

An Introduction to MBTI

The Myers-Briggs Type Indicator Instrument (MBTI) is currently the world's most popular tool for identifying personality types. The test was created by Katharine Briggs and her daughter Isabel Myers during the 1940s.

Their dream was to design a test that could enable empathy between groups of people, in order to increase productivity at home and the workplace. The test went through a 30-year journey of research and beta practice before finally being published and put to use, for both educational and clinical settings. The two began developing their vision during World War II and the Civil Rights Movement. What they created in the end was a system of yes and no questions, designed to categorize one's character traits into a four-letter acronym. These acronyms do not define a person necessarily or bind them to shackles, but instead they are a method of understanding and explaining social and cognitive behavior.

There are sixteen personality types in total: ENTJ, ENTP, ESTJ, ESTP, ENFJ, ENFP, ESFP, ESFJ, ISTJ, ISTP, INFJ, INFP, INTP, INTJ, ISFP, and ISFJ. Each type has a specific role to play. For example, an ENFP is nicknamed "The Inspirer" because of their natural charisma and their ability to influence the people around them. These types can be simplified by their preference towards introversion or extroversion. Both dichotomies are about energy and where one focuses their attention. An introvert focuses their attention on themselves, while an extrovert focuses on the outside world and the people around them.

These acronyms become more complex when trying to understand the six functions, and the four temperaments. The four temperaments include SP, SJ, NF and NT. SP stands for "sensory perception", SJ means "sensory judgment", NFs are "intuitive feelers", and NTs are "intuitive thinkers". Break them down further, and you have: S (sensing), N (intuition), T (thinking), F (feeling), P (Perceiving), and J (judging).

The Four Dimensions of the MBTI

The MBTI is designed to identify the different dichotomies of cognitive and social behavior in humans. These dichotomies are Introversion vs. Extroversion, Sensing vs. Intuition, Feeling vs. Thinking and Perceiving vs. Judging.

First, let's look at introversion and extroversion. In the final results of the MBTI exam, E or I will be the first letter used to generalize one's behavior. There's only one word needed to summarize the two, and that is *energy.* An extrovert gets energy from socializing with other people. Often stereotyped for being loud and outgoing, they like big crowds and perform better in social situations compared to an introvert. On the other hand, introverts lose energy through prolonged social interactions. They will need time alone to regain themselves. Because of this, they can be seen as antisocial and unconfident.

Sensing vs. Intuition describes how someone makes sense of the world around them. Somebody that processes information based off their five senses (hearing, seeing, tasting, touching, smelling) is considered an S. They prefer concrete and tangible realities: looking at the details of a situation, as opposed to the larger picture. An intuitive describes the world through an unconscious filtering mechanism that adds meaning, creates metaphors and lets them see possibilities in ordinary things. A person possesses both sensing and intuition, although one is stronger than the other. To give an example, imagine that you're looking at a book. What do you see? Generally a sensor spends time carefully observing the cover, the inch-wide spine, the name of the author and the styling of the letters. Meanwhile, an intuitive looks at a book and thinks *story*. They aren't as focused on the psychical details of the book; so much as they are the theory of possibilities that unravel once you open it and start reading.

Feeling vs. Thinking is self-explanatory. If somebody is typed as a feeler they base their decisions in life on personal gut instincts and their own emotional judgment on a subject. Thinkers appreciate logical explanations to a phenomenon. They want to know the verifiable facts, and will base their decisions off of that.

Judgment vs. Perception is based on scheduling, organization, and the speed at which one makes their decisions. A person possesses both a judging function and a perceiving function. Although, just like the other functions, one is more prevalent and used more often in one's daily life than the other. A judgment type enjoys having a planned out routine in life. They do their best working within a schedule and meeting deadlines. They can work quickly to get things done. A perceiver takes life by the hour; they don't enjoy making plans so much as going with the flow. They're still able to meet deadlines just as well as a judging type, but can struggle if having to follow a set routine while getting there.

Why is the Myers-Briggs Type Indicator Significant?

The Myers-Briggs Type Indicator Instrument is significant in that the test bridges the theories about personality type by psychologist Carl Jung into our everyday lives. It helps people in their search for identity and understanding. They wanted to actualize Jung's theories into a practical mechanism that could be used easily, and interpreted by everyday people. In that regard, they achieved their goal.

Over the past four decades, the MBTI has become the go-to tool for understanding a person's personality type. The test enables coherency among employees, and generally, after learning about someone else's type (as well as your own), you're more accepting towards their behavior. The earliest example of the test being used in a job setting was in Japan in 1968, when the translated version of the MBTI Instrument helped tailor employees to the right jobs. Today, the MBTI is sometimes used in marriage counseling, personal therapy, and management practices.

Katharine and Isabel's system has become a community builder, as proven by all the many discussion groups online that focus on typing. One example being "NF Geeks with Dr. Mike", a discussion group on Facebook as well as a YouTube Channel dedicated to understanding the ins-and-outs of each type.

By making the theories of Carl Jung more available to everyday people, Katharine and Isabel opened up new possibilities in the field of psychology. They also increased public interest on the subject, and helped in spreading the knowledge that once belonged to a minority of academics, to the whole world.

Uncovering the "Guardian": Who is an ESTJ?

The Acronym ESTJ stands for Extroverted Sensing Thinking Judging. In a simple way, the ESTJ is what most societies would consider their "model citizen." Words that come to mind when thinking about an ESTJ are: efficiency, organization, leadership, social status, hands-on, and opinionated. To understand the heart of an ESTJ you first have to look at their functions.

• TE (Extroverted Thinking) - This is their dominant function, and the reason why they are attracted to the outside world. Extroverted Thinkers want to understand the world through logic. It allows ESTJs to make impersonal decisions, and with their judging function, to do so in the moment. Such a quality makes ESTJs, by nature, good at debating. Having Extroverted Thinking as a dominant function

13

allows ESTJs to be very political, and voice their opinion without caring about how they will affect other people.

• SI (Introverted Sensing) - An ESTJ's auxiliary function is introverted sensing, which means that their own inner world is understood, observed, and made sense of in a practical way. SI also makes sure that any of the extroverted thinking an ESTJ is doing is grounded in reality.

• TE (Extroverted Intuition) - Extroverted Intuition is an ESTJ's tertiary function. It is less expressed than SI, and unless the situation is dire, most ESTJs leave their subconscious intuitive side alone.

• FI (Introverted Feeling) - Introverted Feeling is an ESTJ's "inferior" function, because it's the one they use the least. Why? Well, because it goes against their dominant function of Extroverted Thinking. The two are complete opposites. Introverted feeling is a sensitive function, more concerned with the feeling of the individual than the feelings of others'; aside from that it deals with emotions, rather than logic.

The ESTJ, as with most SJ individuals, are very structure oriented. They have a very real desire to belong to a group, and when manifesting that desire by their extroverted functions they may take on leadership roles. While less likely to become the head honcho of an organization, they are better at roles within leadership where they don't have to create their own rules. They prefer to protect, and defend the rules of their society, or enforce the rules of their household in a patriarch or a matriarch. Because of that ability ESTJs can be referred to as, "The Guardian".

To some, it can be inspiring seeing an ESTJ at work, in school, or just living their private lives as productively as they always do. This type has a lot of dedication, and being a Judging type; they enjoy planning, and follow through with those plans in a very intense manner. You may see an ESTJ volunteering, or carpooling; always on the lookout for a new task to complete. They are like a train, steam-rolling through one activity to the next. For that reason it's unlikely that you will ever see an ESTJ idling their time away, like a P might do given the opportunity.

Being that ESTJs are sensors with a dominant extroverted function means that they are very aware of what is and what is not considered "normal". ESTJs have a "here-and-now" mindset, and know who is who in their social environment. For that reason, they never have a problem fitting in with the crowd. The only sight more rare than seeing an ESTJ idling in the workplace is seeing an ESTJ who doesn't fit in the mold that their society demands.

Why are ESTJs Indispensable Leaders?

ESTJs are natural leaders. Both in private activities, and at the workplace, they can repeatedly be seen in a position where they are taking charge.

The way an ESTJ will usually lead others in a group environment is by using their dominant extroverted thinking function to make logical, smart decisions for the group to carry out. Basically, their bluntness and strong-headed behavior has them telling people what to do (they're quite good at it), while using their auxiliary function of introverted sensing, they're able to do so in a semi-calm fashion. For that reason, ESTJs are sometimes viewed as a type that possesses a "calm confidence" about them.

The reason that ESTJs are such great leaders is because they pay strong attention to details and are meticulous about perfection. They will motivate the people around them to work just as hard as they are by communicating in a clear and authoritative way. Not only that, but they also stand by their opinions and will fight to keep their dominance in a group.

The 7 Greatest Strengths of an ESTJ

ESTJs possess an armory of great qualities about them. If their type did not exist, one could surely assume that a lot of what holds society in place from a structural standpoint would crumble. These qualities all center on a "SJ" desire for community, and having an active role in that community. They are the kings of the SJ temperament.

1. Leadership

ESTJs are natural born leaders. They are good at giving people orders to follow, and giving people the appropriate orders as well. An ESTJ will not give you a task they don't believe you're capable of succeeding at. Sure, the task may be difficult, and it may require you to push yourself a little bit, but you'll be all the more strong-willed after it's complete. That's what the ESTJ wants. They respect strong-willed people. If someone isn't strong-willed from the start, they will be after the ESTJ is done with them…. Well, either that or broken.

2. Responsibility

ESTJs are very responsible people. As a rule they believe that if you say you will do something, you better well do it. An ESTJ's word is their bond. In school these are the kids that showed up to class on time - all the time - because they believed it was the right thing to do. They believe in exemplifying this responsibility, because it is what makes a group's structure more secure. If there is no one in a position to uphold a certain level of responsibility, an ESTJ will take on that role quite directly; in family gatherings, in a relationship, and at the workplace.

3. Detail-Oriented

ESTJs are very focused in their line of work. They admire an attention to detail, i.e., an ESTJ seeks to understand the smaller details of a story that can sometimes be overlooked. Having introverted sensing can make it feel wrong for them to not know the details. Match that up with their dominant extroverted thinking, and you have a type that feels uncomfortable speaking without knowing the proper information.

4. Honesty

When an ESTJ is talking to someone, they will give their honest opinion. They won't beat around the bush in a conversation, or try voicing their opinion in an easier to take fashion. They prefer skipping to the point and expect that you will do the same. Their type is very blunt, and in situations where being blunt has its payoff; it can be a great quality to have. They believe that being honest is one of the keys to coherency. It also makes for better work. Why lie to someone, if by telling them the truth they will produce a better result the second time around? If an ESTJ is bossing you it's because there is a purpose behind it. They're not telling you the facts to be harsh; they just want you to do better. If an ESTJ told you to mop the entire floor so that the entire black smudge between the tiles is gone and you don't get rid of all the smudge, they will tell you do it again until the floor is spotty white and you can see your face sweating on your reflection.

5. Establishing Order

Because of their judging ability, ESTJs enjoy the times where they're able to organize, and plan. ESTJs organize their world with the same amount of precision, and a knowledgeable placement of where something belongs, that makes up your DNA. Speaking of which, that's a great example. Whatever you believe created you, there must have been an ESTJ involved to organize the cells that made up what you are. Your mouth being in the right alignment, the bones in your fingers placed in order *just like that*. Don't get me wrong, they're not intuitive-they didn't THINK UP this stuff, like "ah man if only this guy could grab that cup. He probably wouldn't look like such a dork in front of the girl he's trying to impress." Instead, they took the blueprint, and somehow got the mass of genes that is your DNA to organize and produce a fully functioning hand. "Hey. HEY! G, what ARE you doing? Go stand next to C. And T, why are you and A over in the corner? Break is in NINE MONTHS PEOPLE!-Get back to work." Without an ESTJ to keep your DNA in order you would probably just be a blob.

6. Determination

ESTJs are very determined people. In their mind, lazy qualities cause people to look down at you; making it harder at getting them to do what you say, and following your lead. Even if the task is strenuous and boring, they will push through. When it comes to their opinions an ESTJ will defend them until there is a substantial amount of evidence to sway their stance.

7. Social Animals

ESTJs are highly social people. They're usually never homebodies, and being extroverted, they feel most comfortable in the company of other people. An ESTJ will often enjoy whatever is popular. They will be interested in sports, the most popular shows, and music. If an ESTJ is new to a social group they will have a natural desire to increase their social standing. That can include going to the right parties, talking to the right people, and showing those people why they (the ESTJ) matter. They can be enthusiastic at times, and if it's noticeable that you are in need of help, an ESTJ will lend a hand.

The 5 Greatest Areas of Improvement for an ESTJ

While ESTJs have many great qualities, especially in the regards to their leadership capabilities, they also have some areas that call for improvement. The irony is that a lot of the qualities that can make an ESTJ so great are also the areas where they could improve as well.

1. Being Judgmental

ESTJs judge people and their opinions too harshly. If someone has something to say that an ESTJ doesn't agree with, they won't think twice before letting all of their thoughts beat the person to a pulp. When it comes to their opinion, an ESTJ can believe their own opinion is better than everyone else's, and unless someone else's opinion can be backed by evidence and quickly; the ESTJ will dismiss it as nonsense. Think of Bill O'Reilly on his T.V. show. Bill (who is an ESTJ) is always getting into arguments with his guests. Even when the guest is making sense, and their opinion is valid, Bill will yell at the guest, calling their opinion dumb for being "inconsiderate" to the facts. Judging also plays in an ESTJ's extreme care for a person's social status. Because ESTJs are so great at knowing what is and is not socially acceptable, they will spend time judging a person who is different from them and the rest of their group. If an ESTJ thinks you're not as popular as they are, they may not even bother talking to you. They will belittle you around their friends and ignore you publically to avoid jeopardizing their social status.

2. Underdeveloped Emotions

No, ESTJs aren't sociopaths (not all of them) and they're not these calculated robots walking among us, (those are NTs - just kidding!) but a serious area of improvement for an ESTJ is that they can have a difficult time trying to express how they feel. It can be hard for any type with a dominant extroverted thinking function to express their emotions because their feelings often cannot be quantified in a factual way. An ESTJ can make listening to a friend express his or her feelings turn into an argument that ends in the ESTJ telling their friend that they are a weakling, and they need to "get over it". Although, don't get the wrong idea. Not every ESTJ is inconsiderate. Most ESTJs can listen to what you are saying, and if they're your friend, give you their feedback-though it may not be the feedback you desire. To give an example, say that you're working at this job and everybody at your job makes you feel like you don't belong. You tell the ESTJ that you hate working at this place and that if the money was not the primary incentive you would quit. An ESTJ response to this problem might be something like: "So what? You're there to make money. Not friends. Do the work, and if you do it better than them, they will shut up." There isn't anything wrong necessarily with that response, although it is lacking by not responding to the feelings that you're expressing. Yes, you work to make money. Although your issue is feeling like you don't belong, and that wasn't addressed. This inability to reason with another person's feelings, as well as learning to understand, and express their own emotions, plays into all the other aspects of improvement that an ESTJ might require.

3. Need to Lead

You could argue that the only reason an ESTJ is such an "indispensable leader", is because they have such a strong, "indispensable" need to be that leader. An ESTJ may be uncomfortable if they're not in control. Somebody could blame it on their ego, but it is merely their functions, i.e., if they see a problem, they want to fix that problem themselves. An ESTJ may leave a group project completely if they're not the one in charge. If placed in a group with an already predetermined leader, the ESTJ could try (and probably succeed) in overshadowing the other person.

4. Unable to go with the Flow

It should be obvious by now, that ESTJs live lives of order. Anytime they are in a situation that could place them out of their schedule, they can become insensitive. For example, a surprise birthday party may not be such a festive night after all. This also can turn into a difficulty in being unable to loosen up. A practical joke by a couple of their friends could be seen as getting made fun of, instead of just playing around. A stop for gas could turn into an angered ESTJ, cursing their car for making them a minute or two late for church.

5. Hating the Unconventional

An ESTJ has a strong love for following tradition. What worked before, is what will work now, is something an ESTJ lives by. They don't approve of trotting away from the beaten trail; even if by doing so, it could take them somewhere great. ESTJs also have a strong appreciation for following family traditions as well. If a family member doesn't show up for a family gathering, an ESTJ might see that as a betrayal, and begin to think negatively about the person. The main reason behind all of this behavior is their intense need for community.

What are Some Common Careers of an ESTJ?

ESTJs enjoy working in areas that give them the power to be in charge over other people. They like to wrap their hands around the needs of a situation, and give people certain tasks accordingly. None of these jobs are set in stone-anyone can be great at whatever it is they want to do; although an ESTJ might feel most comfortable with these jobs that highlight their functions, and their temperament.

• Police Officer- Being a police officer highlights an ESTJ's love for protecting tradition, and the rules of their community. Police officers become well known in their community, and are generally looked upon with some degree of respect and authority. Being that cops are not meant to step outside of the law, this lets the ESTJ have an understanding of what is right and what is wrong. The opportunity gives the ESTJ a sense of power over other people. They can arrest, detain, and give tickets to people who are outside the boundaries of the law. An ESTJ can do all of this while never having to use an intuitive function (which they don't prefer to use). A cop doesn't have to try and think outside of tradition, or outside the box, when determining whether someone deserves an arrest, or a ticket; but they're required to have knowledge about following protocol (the law) and how to properly carry out the arrest, or citation. The writing aspects of a police officer are also fitting. When cops are writing their reports, they are supposed to cover the facts, and provide as much attention to detail as possible.

• Military- Similar to police work, the military gives ESTJs the sense of leadership that they desire. They are working within a hierarchical system, which they will admire, and pay attention to. This hierarchy will be an incentive for the ESTJ to move up through the ranks. The military is not an emotional line of work, and generally relies on concrete facts, as with the police service. There are a lot of SJ-types within the military, so an ESTJ will feel at home being around like-minded people.

• Political office- Now, one could argue that the best people in politics are intuitive because they're able to see certain aspects of the law more broadly than someone with a sensing function. Although, don't discredit the ESTJ. People from this type have a lot of determination, as well as a strong desire to protect what they value. In politics they can be respected, especially if the ESTJ is working within their own community. When it comes to fulfilling the needs that their community demands, an ESTJ can set themselves up for the task, and push for laws that they believe in. In a debate, an ESTJ will provide concrete evidence to support the law, and give reasons that are absolute in their opinion as to why it should be implemented.

•   Judge- Similar to the previous job and furthering to support the idea that an ESTJ's greatest desire is upholding their idea of righteousness being the law. A judge can't adhere to any emotional defense. They are permitted from making decisions based off an emotional appeal. Such a job fits an ESTJ because this type, based off of their functions, lacks an amount of empathy. True, in a personal situation it's important to consider the way another person feels, although when it comes to making cold, factual decisions, based off the evidence of a crime, an ESTJ can do this better than any other type.

•   Working in Finance- ESTJs prefer facts, and logical information. That falls into the category of numbers, and money, and sales. Working with numbers does not bother an ESTJ. In school, math was probably one of their best subjects. In relation to the workforce, they are naturally good at processing mathematical information. Jobs in this category include financial officers and accounting agents.

• Jobs in Business and Marketing- Whether working for a top of the line company, a local business in their community, or even managing a retail store, these are areas where ESTJs can shine, and lead the everyday people. Retail gives the ESTJ the ability to schedule people, placing them in charge of tasks that work directly around the people within their community. They are also proficient in areas of business such as marketing and salesmanship.

• Teaching- While they may not provide the emotional understanding that some students require, ESTJs are good at motivating their students by supplying them with hard work. ESTJ teachers thrive to motivate their kids, specifically by means of turning them into hard workers.

Common Workplace Behaviors of an ESTJ

ESTJs are at their best in leadership positions where they are allowed to use all of their functions to produce a positive result. When at the workplace, an ESTJ will thrive to complete a task as efficiently as possible. They enjoy success, and will work hard to achieve what they desire.

Somebody who is an ESTJ can often be seen taking on as many tasks as they can. What one person might find over encumbering the ESTJ will find that they're at home when taking on these many tasks. While a lot of the time they can work themselves to oblivion, that doesn't imply that the work they produce isn't completed on time and possesses a good quality. Their extroverted thinking has them wanting to know more. Still, because they're sensors, the best way for them to understand how to do a task is by doing it hands-on.

The end result is an ESTJ scheduling themselves to work on three different projects in a single week. This is funny, because it is the exact behavior of their opposite type, the INFP, who will take on multiple tasks at once, although feel weighed down by them because of their dominant introverted feeling function.

When it comes to an ESTJ's coworkers, they probably see the ESTJ as a person of authority, even if the ESTJ is just another sales associate within the same clothing store. Among the other sales associates, the ESTJ will enjoy giving them tasks when they're clueless about what to do. Among their co-workers, the ESTJ may be asked for feedback as to whether they're doing something the right way.

As a manager, an ESTJ will want to hold group meetings constantly to discuss business plans with their employees. They will probably have a set schedule for every meeting, possibly, every morning, an hour before the store opens. This will give the ESTJ the opportunity to let everyone know their specific tasks for the day, and when they're allowed to switch from one task to the other. Another reason to hold meetings would be to discuss any problems with the money, or any other area of business that the ESTJ might be concerned about. During the day, they will spend their time going from their office, to the floor. The ESTJ will pay attention to see if there are any customers who are in need of assistance, while collecting immediate feedback from them. They will also be looking to see the condition of their employees, and try to motivate them to keep working.

Socially, the ESTJ will spend a lot of time talking with their coworkers. If the ESTJ isn't spending time socializing, they will probably start to feel a little miserable as most extroverts would. Usually, there will be small talk about on subjects that include sports, relevant topics in their personal lives, as well as what's happening at work.

The kind of work an ESTJ will prefer to do at their job will usually involve a group of people. They can enjoy being a cashier because it gives them the ability to socialize with their coworkers, the customer (working with their hands to bag, wrap, and price). Or they'll enjoy the stock room, where they will be working with a group of people, and providing physical labor. Although anytime an ESTJ is at work, there's the chance that they are going to be considered bossy. They are especially viewed that way in situations where they aren't the boss, and are giving instructions to people who don't enjoy being told what to do. In that situation, the ESTJ can be loud and furious towards a person who they think isn't doing something, "the right way".

When working on projects an ESTJ will keep in close contact with their partners to ensure they are doing things correctly. They expect devotion, as well as hard work to help complete the assignment. The ESTJ will schedule specific times for people to work, and dates where the group gets together to work at the same time.

Overall, the ESTJ is managing things constantly in the workplace. They have a set amount of tasks they know must be done, and won't stop until the tasks are complete. They will look to see if anybody needs help, or to instruct someone on how to do their job more efficiently. An ESTJ could sometimes be labeled as a workaholic for constantly picking up multiple tasks; which come as a result of them needing constant stimulation, as well as their love for achievement.

ESTJ: Parenting Style and Values

ESTJs believe in hard work, honoring responsibility, and respecting tradition. When parenting, they will try their hardest to make sure their children are shown how to live by these principles, and how to become a successful member of society.

Insubordination is a death threat inside an ESTJ household. At an early age, an ESTJ parent will put their child to work. They will make sure they wash their dishes after eating, clean their room frequently, and help out with family activities, such as gardening, and laying down mulch. Their goal is to create a person capable of doing hard work. An ESTJ will be sure to bring their child to community activities, like going to church, volunteering, or any other event that is age appropriate. Their goal is to have a kid live as actively as they do themselves. Involvement in sports and attending summer camps is essential to ensuring their kid is getting the proper amount of social experience.

Their issues with insubordination are challenged when their child reaches adolescence. These are the rough years for the child of an ESTJ. They might feel alone at home, constantly wanting to be as far from their parents as possible. Although this rebellious nature only causes more stress on their parents, making the ESTJ become stricter. The ESTJ is similar to a boa constrictor-squeezing all the rebelliousness out of their kid until he or she dies (or goes off to college; with college being an absolute, inescapable part of their destiny).

During this time, ESTJs can put a lot of responsibility on their children. In school, their kids are set to such a high standard that achieving adequate grades is only half of the job; participating in school sports and any other extracurricular activity is the rest of the requirement. As soon as their kid is of an age where they can get a paying job, the ESTJ will make them find one. They can be overzealous at times-putting their kids through the ring, but their purpose is to prepare them for the adult world.

Social status is another area that greatly concerns an ESTJ. Parents place an emphasis on making sure their kid's behavior is normal, and they are, to some extent, popular among their social groups. What that entails is going to prom, wearing the right clothing, and dictating whom their child is spending time with.

Even though ESTJs can sometimes be overbearing with their expectations and responsibilities for their kids, they are always consistent. An ESTJ's child will always know what they need to bring to the table, and will often work at meeting their parent's expectations. Later in life the ESTJ simmers their intensity, when they see that their child has grown into a person they're proud to call their kid.

Why Do ESTJs Make Good Friends?

As an ESTJ, loyalty is paramount in all other aspects of friendship. An ESTJ will invite you out if they want to spend some time with you, and they will pay for your ticket at the movies if you don't have the money to spend. In times where you have nobody, an ESTJ will come around and help you out. They're the best friend to call if you need help cleaning out your garage, or are planning to move-basically anything that requires someone's organizational skills.

Motivationally speaking, I don't think there is any other type that's as good as an ESTJ is when it comes to getting you in shape. If you're friends with an ESTJ who hits the gym hard, and you're looking for someone to train with, look no further. Being thinkers, they won't succumb to your emotional pleas to give up, and due to their consistent nature they won't forget about training after a week or so. The ESTJ's naturally determined spirit is able to push you to complete whatever you need to finish. They are not lazy people and won't tolerate any laziness from you. They will remind you to take care of something when it needs to be done, and make sure you're aware of the deadline.

In my opinion, everybody needs an extroverted friend. Reason being is that even if you have a tendency to stay at home or to socialize with the same people every day, having an extroverted friend will get you out of the house, and meet new people (like a lover, perhaps?) An extrovert has a multitude of friends who you will be able to meet and learn more things from. They can help you get out of your comfort zone, and help you build more confidence in social situations. Not only that, but because an ESTJ is a sensor, and such an honest one at that, if you're ever curious as to what a certain someone thinks about you, the ESTJ is more than likely to know. Their honest qualities shine best in these situations, where their knowledge from living in the extroverted world can help answer your curiosities.

ESTJ Romance

In relationships, an ESTJ will value communication and activity. Another important thing for an ESTJ to consider if they are going to have a relationship with somebody is being certain that their special someone can respect the same general values as they do.

An ESTJ in a relationship is going to be very active by making sure that there is always something for the two of them to do. They will not hate rainy days where they can't do much, although it may dampen their spirits. For an ESTJ the idea of staying home, in bed, with your significant other, just doesn't sound appealing. There is always something that will worry them in the back of their minds: did I leave the water running? Are there any dishes I can do? How's the living room look? Are the fences for the garden holding up? Even if there aren't any special plans for the day, like going on a date or meeting with family and friends, an ESTJ is going to push for productivity.

During these times, they expect their significant other to do something too, of some equal measure (like trimming the hedges or mowing the lawn).

In marriage, the ESTJ will make sure they are eating dinner regularly. Dinner is a set event that takes place at the same time, every day. The ESTJ will wake up early, to begin their day working. It may sound like slave labor to some more laidback types (especially when realizing that an ESTJ will want to do all of this stuff on their days off, and, after they get home from work as well.) They like to have a strong understanding for what each partner is going to take care of: Who will do the dishes? Who barbeques? - Stuff like that.

Socially, the ESTJ will want to bring their partner with them almost everywhere they go-especially traditional places, such as attending a wedding.

The best types for an ESTJ to date would be anyone who shares the same sensing function as they do. Whether that sensing function should be extroverted (objective) or introverted (subjective) is debatable, but by dating a sensor they ensure their partner is seeing the world through similar enough goggles. Dating an intuitive could prove troubling being that they don't process information the same way as an ESTJ does. Sticking to a type with a similar SJ temperament is probably the safest option. Here's a list of good romantic options: ESFJ, ISTJ, ISFJ, ISTP, ISFP, and ESTJ. The list is in the order I think is best.

Now you may be wondering: why would a fellow ESTJ be in the back of the list? Well, the issue with dating someone from the same type is that while sure, communication will not be an issue; there is very little opportunity for growth. If an ESTJ were to date another ESTJ they may never develop in areas that prove the most challenging for them, like expressing emotions. The safest option would be the ESFJ. Generally, the ESFJ can be considered the same type. They have two similarities: both share the same auxiliary function (introverted sensing), and they're dominant functions are both judging functions that focus on the external world. The only difference being that one follows their emotions, while the other chooses logic. An ESTJ / ESFJ couple will enjoy the same kinds of activities such as sports, volunteering, and having a busy social life. The two share an equal liking for community and subordination.

Weaknesses

• If an ESTJ is over at your house, and there's something they find irritable, like a messy room, a couple missed calls from your parents or an unpaid speeding ticket, they can be a little overzealous when explaining all the "bad decisions" that you're making.

• An ESTJ can be more than a little bossy in situations when you really just want them to shut up -

or leave you alone. If an ESTJ doesn't like the people you're hanging around, they may try and control your life, and stop you from spending time with them.

• Feelers can have a hard time being in a relationship with an ESTJ, because of their inability to respond correctly to emotions. In an argument, an ESTJ will focus on what actually happened, instead of the way something made you feel. While they can try their best to relate with your emotions, getting a good response from them may be difficult.

• A common problem ESTJs face is their inability to stop being productive. Most likely, the ESTJ finds some sort of passion in whatever it is they do. Hence, it can be difficult for them to take their mind away from something they find rewarding. As a reference, the protagonist, Nicholas Angel (an ESTJ), of the British comedy, *Hot Fuzz*, ruined his relationship because he could never stop thinking about his job.

Strengths

•   An ESTJ will always be very loyal to their partner and stand behind them in situations where they have to. You never have to worry about an ESTJ male not making you feel "protected" or, if it's a woman, her not being there to take care of you.

•   In times when you're confused about what you should do, your ESTJ partner will be there to remind you what is and isn't, important. They can offer great practical advice to get some people out a jam.

7 Actionable Steps for Overcoming Your Weaknesses as an ESTJ

The weaknesses that an ESTJ might have are often pretty clear to see. For most their weaknesses can include: having trouble relating to emotions, being inconsiderate to different opinions, bossiness/an urge to control people, disliking/judging people and experiences that are "different" or "weird", being incapable of thinking outside the box, and feeling unable to relax. Those are some common issues that you, as an ESTJ, might be experiencing. So what are some actionable steps that can be taken to help you overcome these problems?

1. Spend Time around Different People

It's always good to understand how other people are experiencing the world. If you start hanging around other people and listening to what they have to say about the things they care for, you can improve two issues: being inconsiderate of different opinions, and having trouble relating to how other people are feeling. If you stop worry about what you think is right and wrong and try to see things from other perspectives, you will be a more successful human being in the long run.

2. Participate in Activities that Stimulate Emotion

It's no surprise to you anymore, when someone says you should be more in touch with your emotions. Now don't take it personally-you don't need to change who you are or anything-although it wouldn't hurt trying to develop a better understanding of what it's like to feel. Write poetry, paint, listen to music that pulls on your heartstrings, watch an emotional movie, or a documentary about rhino's being poached to extinction. When you're expressing yourself through the arts, or in conversation, be sure to let it all out. Try expressing your opinions, your thoughts-anything that may be bottled up inside-let it free. Try remembering a time when somebody did something that hurt your feelings. Even if you can't understand it, in time it will make more sense.

3. Understand Before You Judge

As an ESTJ it's probably very easy for you to come to quick decisions about something, before you know the entire story. It doesn't always matter who is right or who is wrong in an argument. What matters is that the both of you come out of it learning something new. How many times have you looked at somebody, or heard a fraction of what they're saying, before you started judging them? Next time stop yourself and listen to everything they have to say.

4. Judge Yourself as You Judge Others

Be humble. Think humbly. Not everyone is an evil person and believe it or not, a lot of people are just like you. If you're going to judge someone while they're telling you something, you better believe they will do the same thing every time you open your own mouth. Bob Marley put it great in his song *Could You Be Loved?* When he said, "When you point your fingers, someone else is judging you!" He also said, "Judge not, before you judge yourself!" Try to live by those words, and realize that you're not as perfect as you may think. We are all trying to be better than we actually are, so accept that you're not perfect, and focus on how to make yourself more awesome, instead of criticizing other people.

5. Learn How to Follow

Some of the best leaders started out as followers. If you think about it, George Washington never started out as a General; it took him awhile. Do you think he could have possibly known how to command a group of farmers to soldier if he'd never spent time as a lowly recruit himself? There are so many over-confident ESTJs out there who think they can lead a group of people, or know what it takes to be the manager after their first month at a new job. Remember that things take time.

6. Starve the Impulse to Control

You may think you know what's best for someone, although your mind is a mess, and you're only seeing what's best for them from your own ideas of right and wrong. So relax and stop trying to control what other people are doing; who they spend their time with, and what they like to do. Your opinion and beliefs are what work for you and you alone. They're what make you special. And just as you're entitled to live how you like, so are other people. The next time someone says or does something that you disagree with, walk away before you get ugly, and take a chill pill.

7. Be an Introvert

The words, "I'm alone" can be scary if you're extroverted. You're constantly relying on feedback from other people to assure yourself that you're doing what's right. That's absolutely normal, but taking some time away to be on your own is something any healthy person will do from time-to-time. Time spent in solitude gives you a chance to rethink the decisions you've made, and how you can do things better the next time around.

The 10 Most Influential ESTJs We Can Learn From

1. Sonia Sotomayor

Sonia is a Supreme Court Justice in the United States Supreme Court. She's the first Latino woman to hold a position in the court. Sonia herself identifies as an STJ. She is an independent, strong-willed individual, who prides life, fair judgment, and hard work. Although, she breaks the stereotypical mold that ESTJs lack an ability to express and understand their emotions. As a judge, Sonia can sometimes be conflicted by wanting to follow her heart, and wanting to establish the law in a court case.

2. Bill O'Reilly

Unlike Sonia who appears to have developed her emotions more thoroughly, Bill is more of a hot-head. Although he's not a supreme dictator and isn't responsible for the mass murdering of thousands, he's a good example of an ESTJ who's trying to do good things. He represents the community of conservatives in the United States. The fact that the values he represents, and talks about on his show, are so stereotypically ESTJ (e.g the importance of family, religion, and community) and the way he defends these principles like a zealot, supports the idea that he embodies the "Guardian" all too well. This is a man who can't be shaken, and is prone to confrontation. In that regard we are able to get a visual of how an ESTJ will react when you push their buttons. If you can learn anything from Bill, it's that voicing your opinion is generally a good idea. Although listening to others and understanding the opposite side of an argument is just as important. As an ESTJ, he is judgmental, prone to prejudice, and known for giving oversimplified (biased) summarizations of opinions that go against his own.

3. Dr. Phil

Most likely you've seen, or heard of the successful talk show, *Dr. Phil*. His real name is (Dr.) Phillip C. McGraw. Dr. Phil reminds me more of Sonia Sotomayor, in that both of these ESTJs seem to have developed their emotions successfully. He embodies that "calm confidence" ESTJs are known for having, by rarely freaking-out on his guests and providing a clear, focused response to their dilemmas. He represents the ESTJs who pursue careers in psychology; especially the ones landing a job where they can focus on traditional values, by helping families get through their problems.

4. Muhammad

All personal opinions aside, the man responsible for the foundation of one of the world's most popular religion, is undoubtedly, a person of influence. His leadership style combined authority and gentleness. He strived to use his rhetoric skills to instill values of kindness, modesty, justice, liberty and gentility. Muhammad never elevated himself over others and his followers respected, obeyed and loved him because of his humble, kind, patient and tolerant ways. He was convinced in the message of truth he preached and this enabled him to become the great leader we have come to know.

5. Alec Baldwin

Baldwin is an influence for the young, aspiring actors, and workaholics alike; that the harder you work, the more success you will have. He has a strong sense of responsibility and a hunger for achievement. Baldwin believes in government, i.e., for people to follow the law.

6. Augusto Pinochet

Pinochet was the Dictator of Chile from 1974 to 1990. Pinochet was fascist and represented how an ESTJ can sometimes only develop their negative attributes. His desire to have supreme control over other people highlights those attributes. He denied his people popular sovereignty, and broke multiple human rights violations by implementing death camps, refusing elections, and using secret police.

7. Henry Ford

Henry Ford was the founder of Ford Motors. Like so many ESTJs in the business world, he created his own company, which became a success. Ford was an extremely disciplined worker; he would work for hours on end to meet his expectations for himself. He represents the ESTJ's need to achieve their dreams. Unlike an INFP, who can often spend all day dreaming about accomplishing something, the ESTJ feels compelled to act.

8. Michelle Obama

Michelle has been praised by her husband for always standing by his side. Her loyalty to him as First Lady is noticeable; you can tell that she has his back on most decisions. Michelle's the classic case of an ESTJ wife, dedicated to helping her husband, and supporting their children. She's firm, although calm, and confident.

9. Emma Watson

Ms. Harry Potter, and most recently, the feminist ambassador to the United Nations: Emma Watson is probably the most influential ESTJ female figure for young girls at the moment. She's strong-willed, independent, and has been called "efficient" by the people around her.

10. Billy Graham

Graham is a Christian Evangelist, known for his absoluteness in religion. He used the power of radio broadcasting, and television to become one of the most influential evangelists of our time. He's radical and spent much of his life preaching all over the United States, and internationally, going on an ESTJ "crusade" to spread his opinions to millions of people. He was close friends with President Nixon during his time in office and stood by his side during the Watergate Scandal.

Conclusion

Now, as we conclude this book, you should have a general understanding of the ESTJ personality type. Let's review some key areas:

What is an ESTJ?

ESTJ stands for Extroverted, Sensing, Thinking, Judging. Someone who associates themselves with this type will probably exhibit very social characteristics. They will enjoy the company of others, prefer logic over emotions, and will follow a schedule in their personal lives, and at work.

What are some good traits?

- Good leaders
- Loyal friends
- Strong-willed

What are some areas that need improvement?

- Being judgmental
- Needs to be in charge

- Likes to control others

If you're an ESTJ the road ahead could look foggy, or clear. It all depends on how the information provided within this book series has affected you. Hopefully, you feel more confident in who you are, and, if you were lost, have found something that will get you back on track. Now that you know you are an ESTJ, do you feel more self-assured in your actions? Do you have a general idea of the things you may need to work on? As an ESTJ, you're able to accomplish so many things-basically anything you put your mind to. The road ahead may be challenging for those people planning to work out their problems, but being that your type is so relentless, there's no doubt that you can get the job done.

Your goal should be to implement what you have learned about your type into your everyday life. All you have to remember is to take things easy sometimes. When planning out a day with your friends, the only real plan you need is the one where you're having fun. Do not become frustrated when a situation slips out of your control, just take a step back, and simmer down. Remember that you lose the argument as soon as you let your anger get the best of you. Spend time getting to know your emotional side, not overly so, just enough that you're bluntness will come across more and be appreciated as honesty.

Final Word/About the Author

I was born and raised in Norwalk, Connecticut. Growing up, I could often be found spending afternoons reading in the local public library about management techniques and leadership styles, along with overall outlooks towards life. It was from spending those afternoons reading about how others have led productive lives that I was inspired to start studying patterns of human behavior and self-improvement. Usually I write works around sports to learn more about influential athletes in the hopes that from my writing, you the reader can walk away inspired to put in an equal if not greater amount of hard work and perseverance to pursue your goals. However, I began writing about psychology topics such as the Myers Brigg Type Indicator so that I could help others better understand why they act and think the way they do and how to build on their strengths while also identifying their weaknesses. If you enjoyed

ESTJ: Understanding & Relating with the Guardian, please leave a review! Also, you can read more of my works on *How to be Witty, How to be Likeable, Bargain Shopping, Productivity Hacks, Morning Meditation, Becoming a Father,* and *33 Life Lessons: Success Principles, Career Advice & Habits of Successful People* in the Kindle Store.

Like what you read?

If you love books on life, basketball, or productivity, check out my website at claytongeoffreys.com to join my exclusive list where I let you know about my latest books. Aside from being the first to hear about my latest releases, you can also download a free copy of *33 Life Lessons: Success Principles, Career Advice & Habits of Successful People.* See you there!

16589072R00043

Printed in Great Britain
by Amazon